cloverleaf books™

Nature's Patterns

Do Chicks Ask for Snacks?

Noticing Animal Behaviors

Martha E. H. Rustad

illustrated by Mike Moran

M MILLBROOK PRESS · MINNEAPOLIS

For Ethan and Elijah,
from Auntie Martha—M.E.H.R.

For James—M.M.

Millbrook Press
A division of Lerner Publishing Group, Inc.
241 First Avenue North
Minneapolis, MN 55401 USA

For reading levels and more information, look up this title at
www.lernerbooks.com.

Main body text set in Slappy Inline 18/28.
Typeface provided by T26.

Library of Congress Cataloging-in-Publication Data

Rustad, Martha E. H. (Martha Elizabeth Hillman), 1975- author.
    Do chicks ask for snacks? : noticing animal behaviors / by
Martha E. H. Rustad.
        p. cm. — (Cloverleaf books. Patterns)
    Summary: "An introduction to animal behavior"— Provided
by publisher.
    Audience: Ages 5–8.
    Audience: K to grade 3.
    Includes bibliographical references and index.
    ISBN 978-1-4677-8558-7 (lb : alk. paper) —
ISBN 978-1-4677-8603-4 (pb : alk. paper) —
ISBN 978-1-4677-8604-1 (eb pdf)
    1. Animal behavior–Juvenile literature. [1. Animals—Habits
and behavior.] I. Title.
QL751.5.R882 2015
591.5—dc23   2014040980

Manufactured in the United States of America
1 – BP – 7/15/15

TABLE OF CONTENTS

Chapter One
What Do Animals Do?

Our class is going on a field trip to the zoo! We have a job to do while we're there. Ms. McLean has asked us to observe the animals' behavior.

"Does *behavior* mean whether animals follow the rules?" Henry asks.

"No!" Jayla laughs. "I think it means what someone does, like **eating** and **playing**."

"Right," our teacher says. "And flying or making noises. What does *observe* mean?"

"To watch something closely," Lila says.

We make a chart to record, or keep track of, animal behaviors we see.

ANIMAL				
Making Noise				
Eating				
Playing				
Walking				
Flying				
Swimming				
Other				

"Welcome to the zoo!" says our guide, Mr. Sato. He's a zookeeper. He tells us his job is to take care of animals. He also teaches zoo visitors.

"I can't wait to see the tigers!" says Savannah.

"I have a surprise for you," Mr. Sato says. **"A tiger cub!"** The baby tiger makes a scratchy meow. The mother tiger feeds it.

Tiger cubs play and pounce, just like kittens.

Next, we walk to the **zebra** exhibit.

"Zigzag is our youngest zebra. He's only one month old," Mr. Sato says. Zigzag whinnies. His mother feeds him.

"Hey, that's just like my baby brother!" Tonia says. "He cries, and Dad feeds him!"

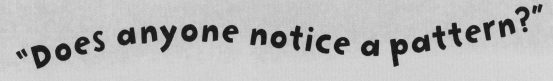

"Does anyone notice a pattern?"

Ms. McLean asks. "That's something that happens over and over."

Max says, "I do! Babies make noises, and parents feed them."

	TIGER	ZEBRA
Making Noise	X	X
Eating	X	X
Walking	X	X

Zebra foals drink milk from their mothers until they are about one year old.

Time for our snack break! We sit under some trees.

"I hear a baby bird cheeping," Raj says.

Ms. McLean asks, "Can you figure out where it's coming from?"

We find the nest. A robin feeds worms to its chicks.

"Is it OK to add *robin* to our animal behavior chart?" Henry asks.

Jayla pipes up, "Hey, it fits the **pattern!** The baby makes a noise and gets fed."

Max says, "We see that **pattern** over and over and over again!"

	ROBIN	
Making Noise	X	
Eating	X	
Flying	X	

Robins feed their chicks worms, insects, and fruit.

Chapter Three

Time to Learn

At the next exhibit, **we watch river otters swim.**

"Look at them dive underwater!" Lila says.

Mr. Sato tells us their parents taught them to swim when they were two months old. Young otters also learn to dive and catch prey.

Then we move on to the raccoon exhibit. We watch furry raccoons play.

"Kits stay with their mothers for about a year," Mr. Sato says. "They learn how to find food and how to stay safe."

	OTTER	RACCOON
Eating		X
Playing		X
Swimming	X	

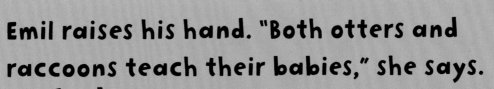

Emil raises his hand. "Both otters and raccoons teach their babies," she says. "Good observation!" says Ms. McLean.

Next, we watch young lions play.

"Look at them pounce!" Raj says. "Just like my cat!"

We learn that lion cubs practice hunting. In the wild, they hunt prey.

We walk over to the chimpanzees. "Young chimps learn to use tools from adult chimps," Mr. Sato says.

Prey is any animal that's eaten by another animal.

"Wait. They use tools? Like hammers?" Savannah asks.

"Not exactly," Ms. McLean smiles.

The zookeeper explains, "They hit nutshells with rocks to crack them open. They also use long sticks to catch ants."

Ms. McLean points out a **pattern**: young animals learn from adult animals.

"Just like kids learn from teachers at school!" Tonia says.

Chapter Four

Helping the Group

Ms. McLean says, "Let's go see the elephants!"

We learn that elephants live in family groups. Wild elephants travel far together to find food.

"They must eat a lot!" Emil says. "Look how huge they are!"

"If a predator comes," Mr. Sato says, "adult elephants make a circle around the young to protect them."

"Cool! They help each other stay safe," Henry says.

	LION	CHIMP	ELEPHANT
			X
Eating			
Playing	X		X
Walking			
Sitting		X	
Other		X	

Elephants keep growing bigger all through their lives. The largest elephants weigh about 9 tons (8 metric tons). That is as much as two large pickup trucks!

The capuchin monkeys are next. **"I love monkeys!"** Emil says. "They're so funny!"

"Why is that monkey picking at the other one?" Lila asks.

"They're grooming each other," Mr. Sato says. He tells us they pick bugs off each other's fur—and eat them!

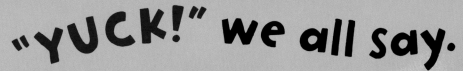

"YUCK!" we all say.

"They do that to help each other stay clean," Ms. McLean says.

"Ms. McLean, another pattern!" says Raj. "Elephants and monkeys both live in groups."

"And they all help take care of others!" Tonia adds.

"Very good!" our teacher says.

Our zoo trip is almost over.

"What do we say to our guide?" Ms. McLean asks.

Together we say, "Thank you, Mr. Sato!"

Back at our classroom, we talk about our trip.

"We saw lots of patterns in animal behavior today. Which did you enjoy watching most?" our teacher asks.

Max says, "When the animals helped each other."

"I liked when the babies asked to eat! Meow!" Jayla says.

"Cheep, cheep!" adds Savannah.

"All right, this class is turning into a zoo," says Ms. McLean. "Go outside for recess!"

Wildlife Watching

Observe wildlife in your backyard or at a park. Watch wild animals, such as birds, squirrels, or rabbits. Record their behavior on a chart.

What You Need:
paper
pencil
an adult to help

1) Make a chart like the one on page 5.

ANIMAL				
Making Noise				
Eating				
Playing				
Walking				
Flying				
Swimming				
Other				

2) Find a safe place to watch wildlife. For example, watch birds out your window. Or ask an adult to take you to a park.

3) Sit quietly. Watch carefully. Record what animals you see and what the animals do.

4) Go back another day. Do you see the same animals? Are their behaviors the same or different?

GLOSSARY

behavior: the way a person or animal acts

exhibit: a display of something

foals: baby horses, zebras, or donkeys

groom: to clean an animal's fur

kits: baby raccoons

observe: to look closely at something

pattern: something that is repeated again and again

pounce: to leap or jump suddenly

predator: an animal that hunts and eats other animals

prey: an animal that is eaten by another animal

record: to write something down

BOOKS
Halfmann, Janet. *Animal Teachers.* Maplewood, NJ: Blue Apple, 2014.
Read more about animals learning lessons.

Meister, Cari. *Do You Really Want to Meet an Elephant?* Mankato, MN:
Amicus, 2016.
Read about elephants in zoos and in the wild.

Shaffer, Jody Jensen. *Chimpanzees.* Minneapolis: Abdo, 2014.
Learn about these clever animals to discover more ways in which chimpanzee
behaviors fit patterns.

WEBSITES
EthoSearch
http://www.ethosearch.org/education/sample_datasheets
Print out a chart for recording animal behavior.

ZooBorns
http://www.zooborns.com
Find out about the newest baby animals in zoos.

LERNER e SOURCE™
Expand learning beyond the
printed book. Download free,
complementary educational
resources for this book
from our website,
www.lerneresource.com.